ILLINOIS RULES OF
2018 Edition

Updated through January 1, 2018

Michigan Legal Publishing Ltd.
QUICK DESK REFERENCE SERIES™

WE WELCOME YOUR FEEDBACK: info@michlp.com

ISBN-13: 978-1-64002-035-1

Article I. General Provisions

Rule 101. Scope

These rules govern proceedings in the courts of Illinois to the extent and with the exceptions stated in Rule 1101. A statutory rule of evidence is effective unless in conflict with a rule or a decision of the Illinois Supreme Court.

Adopted September 27, 2010, eff. January 1, 2011. Comment amended Jan. 6, 2015, eff. immediately.

Rule 102. Purpose and Construction

These rules shall be construed to secure fairness in administration, elimination of unjustifiable expense and delay, and promotion of growth and development of the law of evidence to the end that the truth may be ascertained and proceedings justly determined.

Adopted September 27, 2010, eff. January 1, 2011.

Rule 103. Rulings on Evidence

(a) *Effect of Erroneous Ruling.* Error may not be predicated upon a ruling which admits or excludes evidence unless a substantial right of the party is affected, and
   (1) Objection. In case the ruling is one admitting evidence, a timely objection or motion to strike appears of record, stating the specific ground of objection, if the specific ground was not apparent from the context; or
   (2) Offer of Proof. In case the ruling is one excluding evidence, the substance of the evidence was made known to the court by offer or was apparent from the context within which questions were asked.
(b) *Preserving a Claim of Error for Appeal.*
   (1) Civil and Criminal Cases. In civil and criminal trials where the court has not made a previous ruling on the record concerning the admission of evidence, a contemporaneous trial objection or offer of proof must be made to preserve a claim of error for appeal.

(2) Criminal Cases. In criminal trials, once the court rules before or at trial on the record concerning the admission of evidence, a contemporaneous trial objection or offer of proof need not be renewed to preserve a claim of error for appeal.

(3) Civil Cases. In civil trials, even if the court rules before or at trial on the record concerning the admission of evidence, a contemporaneous trial objection or offer of proof must be made to preserve a claim of error for appeal.

(4) Posttrial Motions. In all criminal trials and in civil jury trials, in addition to the requirements provided above, a claim of error must be made in a posttrial motion to preserve the claim for appeal. Such a motion is not required in a civil nonjury trial.

(c) *Record of Offer and Ruling.* The court may add any other or further statement which shows the character of the evidence, the form in which it was offered, the objection made, and the ruling thereon. It may direct the making of an offer in question and answer form.

(d) *Hearing of Jury.* In jury cases, proceedings shall be conducted, to the extent practicable, so as to prevent inadmissible evidence from being suggested to the jury by any means, such as making statements or offers of proof or asking questions in the hearing of the jury.

(e) *Plain Error.* Nothing in this rule precludes taking notice of plain errors affecting substantial rights although they were not brought to the attention of the court.

Adopted September 27, 2010, eff. January 1, 2011. Amended Oct. 15, 2015, eff. immediately.

Rule 104. Preliminary Questions

(a) *Questions of Admissibility Generally.* Preliminary questions concerning the qualification of a person to be a witness, the existence of a privilege, or the admissibility of evidence shall be determined by the court, subject to the provisions of subdivision (b). In making its determination, the court is not bound by the rules of evidence except those with respect to privileges.

(b) *Relevancy Conditioned on Fact.* When the relevancy of evidence depends upon the fulfillment of a condition of fact, the court shall admit it upon, or subject to, the introduction of evidence sufficient to support a finding of the fulfillment of the condition.

(c) *Hearing of Jury.* Hearings on the admissibility of confessions shall in all cases be conducted out of the hearing of the jury. Hearings on other preliminary matters shall be so conducted when the interests of justice require, or when an accused is a witness and so requests.

(d) *Testimony by Accused.* The accused does not, by testifying upon a preliminary matter, become subject to cross-examination as to other issues in the case.

(e) *Weight and Credibility.* This rule does not limit the right of a party to introduce before the jury evidence relevant to weight or credibility.

Adopted September 27, 2010, eff. January 1, 2011.

Rule 105. Limited Admissibility

When evidence which is admissible as to one party or for one purpose but not admissible as to another party or for another purpose is admitted, the court, upon request, shall restrict the evidence to its proper purpose or scope and instruct the jury accordingly.

Adopted September 27, 2010, eff. January 1, 2011.

Rule 106. Remainder of or Related Writings or Recorded Statements

When a writing or recorded statement or part thereof is introduced by a party, an adverse party may require the introduction at that time of any other part or any other writing or recorded statement which ought in fairness to be considered contemporaneously with it.

Adopted September 27, 2010, eff. January 1, 2011.

Article II. Judicial Notice

Rule 201. Judicial Notice of Adjudicative Facts

(a) *Scope of Rule.* This rule governs only judicial notice of adjudicative facts.

(b) *Kinds of Facts.* A judicially noticed fact must be one not subject to reasonable dispute in that it is either (1) generally known within the territorial jurisdiction of the trial court or (2) capable of accurate and ready determination by resort to sources whose accuracy cannot reasonably be questioned.

(c) *When Discretionary.* A court may take judicial notice, whether requested or not.

(d) *When Mandatory.* A court shall take judicial notice if requested by a party and supplied with the necessary information.

(e) *Opportunity to be Heard.* A party is entitled upon timely request to an opportunity to be heard as to the propriety of taking judicial notice and the tenor of the matter noticed. In the absence of prior notification, the request may be made after judicial notice has been taken.

(f) *Time of Taking Notice.* Judicial notice may be taken at any stage of the proceeding.

(g) *Informing the Jury.* In a civil action or proceeding, the court shall inform the jury to accept as conclusive any fact judicially noticed. In a criminal case, the court shall inform the jury that it may, but is not required to, accept as conclusive any fact judicially noticed.

Adopted September 27, 2010, eff. January 1, 2011.

Article III. Presumptions in Civil Actions and Proceedings

Rule 301. Presumptions in General in Civil Actions and Proceedings

In all civil actions and proceedings not otherwise provided for by rule, statute or court decision, a presumption imposes on the party against whom it is directed the burden of going forward with evidence to rebut or meet the presumption, but does not shift to such party the burden of proof in the sense of the risk of nonpersuasion, which remains throughout the trial upon the party on whom it was originally cast.

Adopted September 27, 2010, eff. January 1, 2011.

Article IV. Relevancy and Its Limits

Rule 401. Definition of "Relevant Evidence"

"Relevant evidence" means evidence having any tendency to make the existence of any fact that is of consequence to the determination of the action more probable or less probable than it would be without the evidence.

Adopted September 27, 2010, eff. January 1, 2011.

Rule 402. Relevant Evidence Generally Admissible; Irrelevant Evidence Inadmissible

All relevant evidence is admissible, except as otherwise provided by law. Evidence which is not relevant is not admissible.

Adopted September 27, 2010, eff. January 1, 2011.

Rule 403. Exclusion of Relevant Evidence on Grounds of Prejudice, Confusion, or Waste of Time

Although relevant, evidence may be excluded if its probative value is substantially outweighed by the danger of unfair prejudice, confusion of the issues, or misleading the jury, or by considerations of undue delay, waste of time, or needless presentation of cumulative evidence.

Adopted September 27, 2010, eff. January 1, 2011.

Rule 404. Character Evidence not Admissible to Prove Conduct; Exceptions; Other Crimes

(a) *Character Evidence Generally.* Evidence of a person's character or a trait of character is not admissible for the purpose of proving action in conformity therewith on a particular occasion, except:
   (1) Character of Accused. In a criminal case, evidence of a pertinent trait of character offered by an accused, or by the prosecution to rebut the same;

    (2) Character of Alleged Victim. In a criminal case, and subject to the limitations imposed by section 115-7 of the Code of Criminal Procedure (725 ILCS 5/115-7), evidence of a pertinent trait of character of the alleged victim of the crime offered by an accused, or by the prosecution to rebut the same, or evidence of a character trait of peacefulness of the alleged victim offered by the prosecution in a homicide or battery case to rebut evidence that the alleged victim was the first aggressor;

    (3) Character of Witness. Evidence of the character of a witness, as provided in Rules 607, 608, and 609.

(b) *Other Crimes, Wrongs, or Acts.* Evidence of other crimes, wrongs, or acts is not admissible to prove the character of a person in order to show action in conformity therewith except as provided by sections 115-7.3, 115-7.4, and 115-20 of the Code of Criminal Procedure (725 ILCS 5/115-7.3, 725 ILCS 5/115-7.4, and 725 ILCS 5/115-20). Such evidence may also be admissible for other purposes, such as proof of motive, opportunity, intent, preparation, plan, knowledge, identity, or absence of mistake or accident.

(c) In a criminal case in which the prosecution intends to offer evidence under subdivision (b), it must disclose the evidence, including statements of witnesses or a summary of the substance of any testimony, at a reasonable time in advance of trial, or during trial if the court excuses pretrial notice on good cause shown.

Adopted September 27, 2010, eff. January 1, 2011.

Rule 405. Methods of Proving Character

(a) *Reputation or Opinion.* In all cases in which evidence of character or a trait of character of a person is admissible, proof may be made by testimony as to reputation, or by testimony in the form of an opinion.

(b) *Specific Instances of Conduct.*

    (1) In cases in which character or a trait of character of a person is an essential element of a charge, claim, or defense, proof may also be made of specific instances of that person's conduct; and

(2) In criminal homicide or battery cases when the accused raises the theory of self-defense and there is conflicting evidence as to whether the alleged victim was the aggressor, proof may also be made of specific instances of the alleged victim's prior violent conduct.

Adopted September 27, 2010, eff. January 1, 2011.

Rule 406. Habit; Routine Practice

Evidence of the habit of a person or of the routine practice of an organization, whether corroborated or not and regardless of the presence of eyewitnesses, is relevant to prove that the conduct of the person or organization on a particular occasion was in conformity with the habit or routine practice.

Adopted September 27, 2010, eff. January 1, 2011.

Rule 408. Compromise and Offers to Compromise

(a) *Prohibited Uses.* Evidence of the following is not admissible on behalf of any party, when offered to prove liability for, invalidity of, or amount of a claim that was disputed as to validity or amount, or to impeach through a prior inconsistent statement or contradiction:
   (1) furnishing or offering or promising to furnish--or accepting or offering or promising to accept--a valuable consideration in compromising or attempting to compromise the claim; and
   (2) conduct or statements made in compromise negotiations regarding the claim.
(b) *Permitted Uses.* This rule does not require the exclusion of any evidence otherwise discoverable merely because it is presented in the course of settlement negotiations. This rule also does not require exclusion if the evidence is offered for purposes not prohibited by subdivision (a). Examples of permissible purposes include proving a witness' bias or prejudice; negating an assertion of undue delay; establishing bad faith; and proving an effort to obstruct a criminal investigation or prosecution.

Adopted September 27, 2010, eff. January 1, 2011.

Rule 409. Payment of Medical and Similar Expenses

In addition to the provisions of section 8-1901 of the Code of Civil Procedure (735 ILCS 5/8-1901), evidence of furnishing or offering or promising to pay medical, hospital, or similar expenses occasioned by an injury is not admissible to prove liability for the injury.

Adopted September 27, 2010, eff. January 1, 2011.

Rule 410. Inadmissibility of Pleas, Plea Discussions, and Related Statements

Evidence of a plea discussion or any resulting agreement, plea, or judgment is not admissible in any criminal proceeding against the defendant who made the plea or was a participant in the plea discussions under the following circumstances:
    (1) a plea of guilty which is not accepted or is withdrawn;
    (2) a plea of nolo contendere;
    (3) any statement made in the course of any proceedings under Illinois Supreme Court Rule 402 regarding either of the foregoing pleas; or
    (4) any statement made in the course of a plea discussions which does not result in a plea of guilty, or which results in a plea of guilty which is not accepted or is withdrawn, or which results in a judgment on a plea of guilty which is reversed on direct or collateral review.

Adopted September 27, 2010, eff. January 1, 2011. Amended Oct. 15, 2015, eff. immediately.

Rule 411. Liability Insurance

Evidence that a person was or was not insured against liability is not admissible upon the issue whether the person acted negligently or otherwise wrongfully. This rule does not require the exclusion of evidence of insurance against liability when offered for another purpose, such as proof of agency, ownership, or control, or bias or prejudice of a witness.

Adopted September 27, 2010, eff. January 1, 2011.

Rule 412. Prior Sexual Activity or Reputation as Evidence

Evidence of the sexual activity or reputation of a person alleged to be a victim of a sexual offense is inadmissible:

(a) in criminal cases, as provided for and subject to the exceptions in section 115-7 of the Code of Criminal Procedure of 1963 (725 ILCS 5/115-7);

(b) in civil cases, as provided for and subject to the exceptions in section 8-2801 of the Code of Civil Procedure (735 ILCS 5/8-2801).

Adopted Oct. 15, 2015, eff. immediately.

Rule 413. Evidence of Other Offenses in Criminal Cases

(a) *Evidence in Certain Cases.* In a criminal case for an offense set forth in section 115-7.3 of the Code of Criminal Procedure of 1963 (725 ILCS 5/115-7.3), evidence of the defendant's commission of another offense or offenses set forth in section 115-7.3 is admissible, as provided in section 115-7.3.

(b) *Evidence in Domestic Violence Cases.* In a criminal case for an offense related to domestic violence as set forth in section 115-7.4 of the Code of Criminal Procedure of 1963 (725 ILCS 5/115-7.4), evidence of the defendant's commission of another offense or offenses of domestic violence is admissible, as provided in section 115-7.4.

(c) *Evidence of Prior Convictions.* In a criminal case for the type of offenses set forth in section 115-20 of the Code of Criminal Procedure of 1963 (725 ILCS 5/115-20), evidence of the defendant's conviction for an offense set forth in that section is admissible when the victim is the same person who was the victim of the previous offense that resulted in the conviction of the defendant, as provided in section 115-20.

Adopted Oct. 15, 2015, eff. immediately.

Article V. Privileges

Rule 501. General Rule

Except as otherwise required by the Constitution of the United States, the Constitution of Illinois, or provided by applicable statute or rule prescribed by the Supreme Court, the privilege of a witness, person, government, state, or political subdivision thereof shall be governed by the principles of the common law as they may be interpreted by Illinois courts in the light of reason and experience.

Adopted September 27, 2010, eff. January 1, 2011.

Rule 502. Attorney-Client Privilege and Work Product; Limitations on Waiver

The following provisions apply, in the circumstances set out, to disclosure of a communication or information covered by the attorney-client privilege or work-product protection.

(a) *Disclosure Made in an Illinois Proceeding or to an Illinois Office or Agency; Scope of a Waiver.* When the disclosure is made in an Illinois proceeding or to an Illinois office or agency and waives the attorney-client privilege or work-product protection, the waiver extends to an undisclosed communication or information in any proceeding only if:
   (1) the waiver is intentional;
   (2) the disclosed and undisclosed communications or information concern the same subject matter; and
   (3) they ought in fairness to be considered together.

(b) *Inadvertent Disclosure.* When made in an Illinois proceeding or to an Illinois office or agency, the disclosure does not operate as a waiver in any proceeding if:
   (1) the disclosure is inadvertent;
   (2) the holder of the privilege or protection took reasonable steps to prevent disclosure; and
   (3) the holder promptly took reasonable steps to rectify the error, including (if applicable) following Supreme Court Rule 201(p).

(c) *Disclosure Made in a Federal or Another State's Proceeding or to a Federal or Another State's Office or Agency.* When the disclosure is made in a federal or another state's proceeding or to a federal or another state's office or agency and is not the subject of a court order concerning waiver, the disclosure does not operate as a waiver in an Illinois proceeding if the disclosure:

   (1) would not be a waiver under this rule if it had been made in an Illinois proceeding; or

   (2) is not a waiver under the law governing the federal or state proceeding where the disclosure occurred.

(d) *Controlling Effect of a Court Order.* An Illinois court may order that the privilege or protection is not waived by disclosure connected with the litigation pending before the court--in which event the disclosure is also not a waiver in any other proceeding.

(e) *Controlling Effect of a Party Agreement.* An agreement on the effect of disclosure in an Illinois proceeding is binding only on the parties to the agreement, unless it is incorporated into a court order.

(f) *Definitions.* In this rule:

   (1) "attorney-client privilege" means the protection that applicable law provides for confidential attorney-client communications; and

   (2) "work-product protection" means the protection that applicable law provides for tangible material (or its intangible equivalent) prepared in anticipation of litigation or for trial.

Adopted Nov. 28, 2012, eff. Jan. 1, 2013.

Article VI. Witnesses

Rule 601. General Rule of Competency

Every person is competent to be a witness, except as otherwise provided by these rules, by other rules prescribed by the Supreme Court, or by statute.

Adopted September 27, 2010, eff. January 1, 2011.

Rule 602. Lack of Personal Knowledge

A witness may not testify to a matter unless evidence is introduced sufficient to support a finding that the witness has personal knowledge of the matter. Evidence to prove personal knowledge may, but need not, consist of the witness' own testimony. This rule is subject to the provisions of Rule 703, relating to opinion testimony by expert witnesses.

Adopted September 27, 2010, eff. January 1, 2011.

Rule 603. Oath or Affirmation

Before testifying, every witness shall be required to declare that the witness will testify truthfully, by oath or affirmation, administered in a form calculated to awaken the witness' conscience and impress the witness' mind with the duty to do so.

Adopted September 27, 2010, eff. January 1, 2011.

Rule 604. Interpreters

An interpreter is subject to the provisions of these rules relating to qualification as an expert and the administration of an oath or affirmation to make a true translation.

Adopted September 27, 2010, eff. January 1, 2011.

Rule 605. Competency of Judge as Witness

The judge presiding at the trial may not testify in that trial as a witness. No objection need be made in order to preserve the point.

Adopted September 27, 2010, eff. January 1, 2011.

Rule 606. Competency of Juror as Witness

(a) *At the Trial.* A member of the jury may not testify as a witness before that jury in the trial of the case in which the juror is sitting. If the juror is called so to testify, the opposing party shall be afforded an opportunity to object out of the presence of the jury.

(b) *Inquiry Into Validity of Verdict or Indictment.* Upon an inquiry into the validity of a verdict or indictment, a juror may not testify as to any matter or statement occurring during the course of the jury's deliberations or to the effect of anything upon that or any other juror's mind or emotions as influencing the juror to assent to or dissent from the verdict or indictment or concerning the juror's mental processes in connection therewith. But a juror may testify (1) whether any extraneous prejudicial information was improperly brought to the jury's attention, (2) whether any outside influence was improperly brought to bear upon any juror, or (3) whether there was a mistake in entering the verdict onto the verdict form. A juror's affidavit or evidence of any statement by the juror may not be received concerning a matter about which the juror would be precluded from testifying.

Adopted September 27, 2010, eff. January 1, 2011.

Rule 607. Who May Impeach

The credibility of a witness may be attacked by any party, including the party calling the witness, except that the credibility of a witness may be attacked by the party calling the witness by means of a prior inconsistent statement only upon a showing of affirmative damage. The foregoing exception does not apply to statements admitted pursuant to Rules 801(d)(1)(A), 801(d)(1) (B), 801(d)(2), or 803.

Adopted September 27, 2010, eff. January 1, 2011.

Rule 608. Evidence of Character of Witness for Truthfulness or Untruthfulness

The credibility of a witness may be attacked or supported by evidence in the form of opinion or reputation, but subject to these limitations: (1) the evidence may refer only to character for truthfulness or untruthfulness, and (2) evidence of truthful character is admissible only after the character of the witness for truthfulness has been attacked by opinion or reputation evidence or otherwise.

Adopted September 27, 2010, eff. January 1, 2011. Amended Jan. 6, 2015, eff. immediately.

Rule 609. Impeachment by Evidence of Conviction of Crime

(a) *General Rule.* For the purpose of attacking the credibility of a witness, evidence that the witness has been convicted of a crime, except on a plea of nolo contendere, is admissible but only if the crime, (1) was punishable by death or imprisonment in excess of one year under the law under which the witness was convicted, or (2) involved dishonesty or false statement regardless of the punishment unless (3), in either case, the court determines that the probative value of the evidence of the crime is substantially outweighed by the danger of unfair prejudice.

(b) *Time Limit.* Evidence of a conviction under this rule is not admissible if a period of more than 10 years has elapsed since the date of conviction or of the release of the witness from confinement, whichever is the later date.

(c) *Effect of Pardon, Annulment, or Certificate of Rehabilitation.* Evidence of a conviction is not admissible under this rule if (1) the conviction has been the subject of a pardon, annulment, certificate of rehabilitation, or other equivalent procedure, and (2) the procedure under which the same was granted or issued required a substantial showing of rehabilitation or was based on innocence.

(d) *Juvenile Adjudications.* Evidence of juvenile adjudications is generally not admissible under this rule. The court may, however, allow evidence of a juvenile adjudication of a witness other than the accused if conviction of the offense would be admissible to attack the credibility of an adult and the court is satisfied that admission in evidence is necessary for a fair determination of the issue of guilt or innocence.

(e) *Pendency of Appeal.* The pendency of an appeal therefrom does not render evidence of a conviction inadmissible. Evidence of the pendency of an appeal is admissible.

Adopted September 27, 2010, eff. January 1, 2011. Comment amended Jan. 6, 2015, eff. immediately.

Rule 610. Religious Beliefs or Opinions

Evidence of the beliefs or opinions of a witness on matters of religion is not admissible for the purpose of showing that by reason of their nature the witness' credibility is impaired or enhanced.

Adopted September 27, 2010, eff. January 1, 2011.

Rule 611. Mode and Order of Interrogation and Presentation

(a) *Control by Court.* The court shall exercise reasonable control over the mode and order of interrogating witnesses and presenting evidence so as to (1) make the interrogation and presentation effective for the ascertainment of the truth, (2) avoid needless consumption of time, and (3) protect witnesses from harassment or undue embarrassment.

(b) *Scope of Cross-Examination.* Cross-examination should be limited to the subject matter of the direct examination and matters affecting the credibility of the witness, which include matters within the knowledge of the witness that explain, qualify, discredit or destroy the witness's direct testimony. The court may, in the exercise of discretion, permit inquiry into additional matters as if on direct examination.

(c) *Leading Questions.* Leading questions should not be used on the direct examination of a witness except as may be necessary to develop the witness' testimony. Ordinarily leading questions should be permitted on cross-examination. When a party calls a hostile or an unwilling witness or an adverse party or an agent of an adverse party as defined by section 2-1102 of the Code of

Civil Procedure (735 ILCS 5/2-1102), interrogation may be by leading questions.

Adopted September 27, 2010, eff. January 1, 2011. Amended Oct. 15, 2015, eff. immediately.

Rule 612. Writing Used to Refresh Memory

If a witness uses a writing to refresh memory for the purpose of testifying, either--
  (1) while testifying, or
  (2) before testifying, an adverse party is entitled to have the writing produced at the hearing, to inspect it, to cross-examine the witness thereon, and to introduce in evidence for the purpose of impeachment those portions which relate to the testimony of the witness. If it is claimed that the writing contains matters not related to the subject matter of the testimony the court shall examine the writing in camera, excise any portions not so related, and order delivery of the remainder to the party entitled thereto. Any portion withheld over objections shall be preserved and made available to the appellate court in the event of an appeal. If a writing is not produced or delivered pursuant to order under this rule, the court shall make any order justice requires, except that in criminal cases when the prosecution elects not to comply, the order shall be one striking the testimony or, if the court in its discretion determines that the interests of justice so require, declaring a mistrial.

Adopted September 27, 2010, eff. January 1, 2011.

Rule 613. Prior Statements of Witnesses

(a) *Examining Witness Concerning Prior Statement.* In examining a witness concerning a prior statement made by the witness, whether written or not, the statement need not be shown nor its contents disclosed to the witness at that time, but on request the same shall be shown or disclosed to opposing counsel.
(b) *Extrinsic Evidence of Prior Inconsistent Statement of Witness.* Extrinsic evidence of a prior inconsistent statement by a witness

is not admissible unless the witness is first afforded an opportunity to explain or deny the same and the opposing party is afforded an opportunity to interrogate the witness thereon, or the interests of justice otherwise require. This provision does not apply to statements of a party-opponent as defined in Rule 801(d)(2).

(c) *Evidence of Prior Consistent Statement of Witness.* A prior statement that is consistent with the declarant-witness's testimony is admissible, for rehabilitation purposes only and not substantively as a hearsay exception or exclusion, when the declarant testifies at the trial or hearing and is available to the opposing party for examination concerning the statement, and the statement is offered to rebut an express or implied charge that:

(i) the witness acted from an improper influence or motive to testify falsely, if that influence or motive did not exist when the statement was made; or

(ii) the witness's testimony was recently fabricated, if the statement was made before the alleged fabrication occurred.

Adopted September 27, 2010, eff. January 1, 2011. Amended Jan. 6, 2015, eff. immediately; Oct. 15, 2015, eff. immediately.

Rule 614. Calling and Interrogation of Witnesses by Court

(a) *Calling by Court.* The court may, on its own motion or at the suggestion of a party, call witnesses, and all parties are entitled to cross-examine witnesses thus called.

(b) *Interrogation by Court.* The court may interrogate witnesses, whether called by itself or by a party.

(c) *Objections.* Objections to the calling of witnesses by the court or to interrogation by it may be made at the time or at the next available opportunity when the jury is not present.

Adopted September 27, 2010, eff. January 1, 2011.

Rule 615. Exclusion of Witnesses

At the request of a party the court shall order witnesses excluded so that they cannot hear the testimony of other witnesses, and it may make the order of its own motion. This rule does not authorize exclusion of (1) a party who is a natural person, or (2) an officer or employee of a party which is not a natural person designated as its representative by its attorney, or (3) a person whose presence is shown by a party to be essential to the presentation of the party's cause, or (4) a person authorized by law to be present.

Adopted September 27, 2010, eff. January 1, 2011.

Article VII. Opinions and Expert Testimony

Rule 701. Opinion Testimony by Lay Witnesses

If the witness is not testifying as an expert, the witness' testimony in the form of opinions or inferences is limited to those opinions or inferences which are (a) rationally based on the perception of the witness, and (b) helpful to a clear understanding of the witness' testimony or the determination of a fact in issue, and (c) not based on scientific, technical, or other specialized knowledge within the scope of Rule 702.

Adopted September 27, 2010, eff. January 1, 2011.

Rule 702. Testimony by Experts

If scientific, technical, or other specialized knowledge will assist the trier of fact to understand the evidence or to determine a fact in issue, a witness qualified as an expert by knowledge, skill, experience, training, or education, may testify thereto in the form of an opinion or otherwise. Where an expert witness testifies to an opinion based on a new or novel scientific methodology or principle, the proponent of the opinion has the burden of showing the methodology or scientific principle on which the opinion is based is sufficiently established to have gained general acceptance in the particular field in which it belongs.

Adopted September 27, 2010, eff. January 1, 2011.

COMMENT

Rule 702 confirms that Illinois is a Frye state. The second sentence of the rule enunciates the core principles of the Frye test for admissibility of scientific evidence as set forth in *Donaldson v. Central Illinois Public Service Co.*, 199 Ill.2d 63, 767 N.E.2d 314 (2002).

Rule 703. Bases of Opinion Testimony by Experts

The facts or data in the particular case upon which an expert bases an opinion or inference may be those perceived by or made known to the expert at or before the hearing. If of a type reasonably relied upon by experts in the particular field in forming opinions or inferences upon the subject, the facts or data need not be admissible in evidence.

Adopted September 27, 2010, eff. January 1, 2011.

Rule 704. Opinion on Ultimate Issue

Testimony in the form of an opinion or inference otherwise admissible is not objectionable because it embraces an ultimate issue to be decided by the trier of fact.

Adopted September 27, 2010, eff. January 1, 2011.

Rule 705. Disclosure of Facts or Data Underlying Expert Opinion

The expert may testify in terms of opinion or inference and give reasons therefor without first testifying to the underlying facts or data, unless the court requires otherwise. The expert may in any event be required to disclose the underlying facts or data on cross-examination.

Adopted September 27, 2010, eff. January 1, 2011.

Article VIII. Hearsay

Rule 801. Definitions

The following definitions apply under this article:

(a) *Statement.* A "statement" is (1) an oral or written assertion or (2) nonverbal conduct of a person, if it is intended by the person as an assertion.

(b) *Declarant.* A "declarant" is a person who makes a statement.

(c) *Hearsay.* "Hearsay" is a statement, other than one made by the declarant while testifying at the trial or hearing, offered in evidence to prove the truth of the matter asserted.

(d) *Statements Which Are Not Hearsay.* A statement is not hearsay if

  (1) Prior Statement by Witness. In a criminal case, the declarant testifies at the trial or hearing and is subject to cross-examination concerning the statement, and the statement is

    (A) inconsistent with the declarant's testimony at the trial or hearing, and--

      (1) was made under oath at a trial, hearing, or other proceeding, or in a deposition, or

      (2) narrates, describes, or explains an event or condition of which the declarant had personal knowledge, and

        (a) the statement is proved to have been written or signed by the declarant, or

        (b) the declarant acknowledged under oath the making of the statement either in the declarant's testimony at the hearing or trial in which the admission into evidence of the prior statement is being sought or at a trial, hearing, or other proceeding, or in a deposition, or

        (c) the statement is proved to have been accurately recorded by a tape recorder, videotape recording, or any other similar electronic means of sound recording; or

    (B) one of identification of a person made after perceiving the person.

  (2) Statement by Party-Opponent. The statement is offered against a party and is (A) the party's own statement, in

either an individual or a representative capacity, or (B) a statement of which the party has manifested an adoption or belief in its truth, or (C) a statement by a person authorized by the party to make a statement concerning the subject, or (D) a statement by the party's agent or servant concerning a matter within the scope of the agency or employment, made during the existence of the relationship, or (E) a statement by a coconspirator of a party during the course and in furtherance of the conspiracy, or (F) a statement by a person, or a person on behalf of an entity, in privity with the party or jointly interested with the party.

Adopted September 27, 2010, eff. January 1, 2011. Amended Oct. 15, 2015, eff. immediately.

Rule 802. Hearsay Rule

Hearsay is not admissible except as provided by these rules, by other rules prescribed by the Supreme Court, or by statute as provided in Rule 101.

Adopted September 27, 2010, eff. January 1, 2011.

Rule 803. Hearsay Exceptions; Availability of Declarant Immaterial

The following are not excluded by the hearsay rule, even though the declarant is available as a witness:

(1) *Reserved.* [Present Sense Impressions].
(2) *Excited Utterance.* A statement relating to a startling event or condition made while the declarant was under the stress of excitement caused by the event or condition.
(3) *Then Existing Mental, Emotional, or Physical Condition.* A statement of the declarant's then existing state of mind, emotion, sensation, or physical condition (such as intent, plan, motive, design, mental feeling, pain, and bodily health), but not including:
  (A) a statement of memory or belief to prove the fact remembered or believed unless it relates to the

execution, revocation, identification, or terms of declarant's will; or

(B) a statement of declarant's then existing state of mind, emotion, sensation, or physical condition to prove the state of mind, emotion, sensation, or physical condition of another declarant at that time or at any other time when such state of the other declarant is an issue in the action.

(4) *Statements for Purposes of Medical Diagnosis or Treatment.* (A) Statements made for purposes of medical treatment, or medical diagnosis in contemplation of treatment, and describing medical history, or past or present symptoms, pain, or sensations, or the inception or general character of the cause or external source thereof insofar as reasonably pertinent to diagnosis or treatment but, subject to Rule 703, not including statements made to a health care provider consulted solely for the purpose of preparing for litigation or obtaining testimony for trial, or (B) in a prosecution for violation of sections 11-1.20, 11-1.30, 11-1.40, 11-1.50, or 11-1.60 of the Criminal Code of 1961 (720 ILCS 5/11-1.20, 11-1.30, 11-1.40, 11-1.50, 11-1.60), or for a violation of the Article 12 statutes in the Criminal Code of 1961 that previously defined the same offenses, statements made by the victim to medical personnel for purposes of medical diagnoses or treatment including descriptions of the cause of symptom, pain or sensations, or the inception or general character of the cause or external source thereof insofar as reasonably pertinent to diagnosis or treatment.

(5) *Recorded Recollection.* A memorandum or record concerning a matter about which a witness once had knowledge but now has insufficient recollection to enable the witness to testify fully and accurately, shown to have been made or adopted by the witness when the matter was fresh in the witness' memory and to reflect that knowledge correctly.

(6) *Records of Regularly Conducted Activity.* A memorandum, report, record, or data compilation, in any form, of acts, events, conditions, opinions, or diagnoses, made at or near the time by, or from information transmitted by, a person with knowledge, if kept in the course of a regularly

conducted business activity, and if it was the regular practice of that business activity to make the memorandum, report, record or data compilation, all as shown by the testimony of the custodian or other qualified witness, or by certification that complies with Rule 902(11), unless the source of information or the method or circumstances of preparation indicate lack of trustworthiness, but not including in criminal cases medical records. The term "business" as used in this paragraph includes business, institution, association, profession, occupation, and calling of every kind, whether or not conducted for profit.

(7) *Absence of Entry in Records Kept in Accordance With the Provisions of Paragraph (6).* Evidence that a matter is not included in the memoranda reports, records, or data compilations, in any form, kept in accordance with the provisions of paragraph (6), to prove the nonoccurrence or nonexistence of the matter, if the matter was of a kind of which a memorandum, report, record, or data compilation was regularly made and preserved, unless the sources of information or other circumstances indicate lack of trustworthiness.

(8) *Public Records and Reports.* Records, reports, statements, or data compilations, in any form, of public offices or agencies, setting forth (A) the activities of the office or agency, or (B) matters observed pursuant to duty imposed by law as to which matters there was a duty to report, excluding, however, police accident reports and in criminal cases medical records and matters observed by police officers and other law enforcement personnel, unless the sources of information or other circumstances indicate lack of trustworthiness.

(9) *Records of Vital Statistics.* Facts contained in records or data compilations, in any form, of births, fetal deaths, deaths, or marriages, if the report thereof was made to a public office pursuant to requirements of law.

(10) *Absence of Public Record or Entry.* To prove the absence of a record, report, statement, or data compilation, in any form, or the nonoccurrence or nonexistence of a matter of which a record, report, statement, or data compilation, in any form, was regularly made and preserved by a public office or

agency, evidence in the form of a certification in accordance with Rule 902, or testimony, that diligent search failed to disclose the record, report, statement, or data compilation, or entry.

(11) *Records of Religious Organizations.* Statements of births, marriages, divorces, deaths, legitimacy, ancestry, relationship by blood or marriage, or other similar facts of personal or family history, contained in a regularly kept record of a religious organization.

(12) *Marriage, Baptismal, and Similar Certificates.* Statements of fact contained in a certificate that the maker performed a marriage or other ceremony or administered a sacrament, made by a clergyman, public official, or other person authorized by the rules or practices of a religious organization or by law to perform the act certified, and purporting to have been issued at the time of the act or within a reasonable time thereafter.

(13) *Family Records.* Statements of fact concerning personal or family history contained in family Bibles, genealogies, charts, engravings on rings, inscriptions on family portraits, engravings on urns, crypts, or tombstones, or the like.

(14) *Records of Documents Affecting an Interest in Property.* The record of a document purporting to establish or affect an interest in property, as proof of the content of the original recorded document and its execution and delivery by each person by whom it purports to have been executed, if the record is a record of a public office and an applicable statute authorizes the recording of documents of that kind in that office.

(15) *Statements in Documents Affecting an Interest in Property.* A statement contained in a document purporting to establish or affect an interest in property if the matter stated was relevant to the purpose of the document, unless dealings with the property since the document was made have been inconsistent with the truth of the statement or the purport of the document.

(16) *Statements in Ancient Documents.* Statements in a document in existence 20 years or more the authenticity of which is established.

(17) *Market Reports, Commercial Publications.* Market quotations, tabulations, lists, directories, or other published compilations, generally used and relied upon by the public or by persons in particular occupations.

(18) *Reserved.* [Learned Treatises].

(19) *Reputation Concerning Personal or Family History.* Reputation among members of a person's family by blood, adoption, or marriage, or among a person's associates, or in the community, concerning a person's birth, adoption, marriage, divorce, death, legitimacy, relationship by blood, adoption, or marriage, ancestry, or other similar fact of personal or family history.

(20) *Reputation Concerning Boundaries or General History.* Reputation in a community, arising before the controversy, as to boundaries of or customs affecting lands in the community, and reputation as to events of general history important to the community or State or nation in which located.

(21) *Reputation as to Character.* Reputation of a person's character among associates or in the community.

(22) *Judgment of Previous Conviction.* Evidence of a final judgment, entered after a trial or upon a plea of guilty, adjudging a person guilty of a crime punishable by death or imprisonment in excess of one year, to prove any fact essential to sustain the judgment, but not including, when offered by the Government in a criminal prosecution for purposes other than impeachment, judgments against persons other than the accused. The pendency of an appeal may be shown but does not affect admissibility.

(23) *Judgment as to Personal, Family or General History, or Boundaries.* Judgments as proof of matters of personal, family or general history, or boundaries, essential to the judgment, if the same would be provable by evidence of reputation.

(24) *Receipt or Paid Bill.* A receipt or paid bill as prima facie evidence of the fact of payment and as prima facie evidence that the charge was reasonable.

Adopted September 27, 2010, eff. January 1, 2011. Amended April 26, 2012, eff. immediately.

Rule 804. Hearsay Exceptions; Declarant Unavailable

(a) *Definition of Unavailability*. "Unavailability as a witness" includes situations in which the declarant-

    (1) is exempted by ruling of the court on the ground of privilege from testifying concerning the subject matter of the declarant's statement; or

    (2) persists in refusing to testify concerning the subject matter of the declarant's statement despite an order of the court to do so; or

    (3) testifies to a lack of memory of the subject matter of the declarant's statement; or

    (4) is unable to be present or to testify at the hearing because of death or then existing physical or mental illness or infirmity; or

    (5) is absent from the hearing and the proponent of a statement has been unable to procure the declarant's attendance (or in the case of a hearsay exception under subdivision (b)(2), (3), or (4), the declarant's attendance or testimony) by process or other reasonable means.

A declarant is not unavailable as a witness if exemption, refusal, claim of lack of memory, inability, or absence is due to the procurement or wrongdoing of the proponent of a statement for the purpose of preventing the witness from attending or testifying.

(b) *Hearsay Exceptions*. The following are not excluded by the hearsay rule if the declarant is unavailable as a witness:

    (1) Former Testimony. Testimony given as a witness (A) at another hearing of the same or a different proceeding, or in an evidence deposition taken in compliance with law in the course of the same or another proceeding, if the party against whom the testimony is now offered, or, in a civil action or proceeding, a predecessor in interest, had an opportunity and similar motive to develop the testimony by direct, cross, or redirect examination, or (B) in a discovery deposition as provided for in Supreme Court Rule 212(a)(5).

    (2) Statement Under Belief of Impending Death. In a prosecution for homicide, a statement made by a declarant while believing that the declarant's death was imminent,

concerning the cause or circumstances of what the declarant believed to be impending death.

(3) Statement Against Interest. A statement which was at the time of its making so far contrary to the declarant's pecuniary or proprietary interest, or so far tended to subject the declarant to civil or criminal liability, or to render invalid a claim by the declarant against another, that a reasonable person in the declarant's position would not have made the statement unless believing it to be true. A statement tending to expose the declarant to criminal liability and offered in a criminal case is not admissible unless corroborating circumstances clearly indicate the trustworthiness of the statement.

(4) Statement of Personal or Family History.

    (A) A statement concerning the declarant's own birth, adoption, marriage, divorce, legitimacy, relationship by blood, adoption, or marriage, ancestry, or other similar fact of personal or family history, even though declarant had no means of acquiring personal knowledge of the matter stated; or

    (B) a statement concerning the foregoing matters, and death also, of another person, if the declarant was related to the other by blood, adoption, or marriage or was so intimately associated with the other's family as to be likely to have accurate information concerning the matter declared.

(5) Forfeiture by Wrongdoing. A statement offered against a party that has engaged or acquiesced in wrongdoing that was intended to, and did, procure the unavailability of the declarant as a witness.

Adopted September 27, 2010, eff. January 1, 2011.

Rule 805. Hearsay Within Hearsay

Hearsay included within hearsay is not excluded under the hearsay rule if each part of the combined statements conforms with an exception to the hearsay rule provided in these rules.

Adopted September 27, 2010, eff. January 1, 2011.

Rule 806. Attacking and Supporting Credibility of Declarant

When a hearsay statement, or a statement defined in Rule 801(d)(2)(C), (D), (E), or (F), has been admitted in evidence, the credibility of the declarant may be attacked, and if attacked may be supported, by any evidence which would be admissible for those purposes if declarant had testified as a witness. Evidence of a statement or conduct by the declarant at any time, inconsistent with the declarant's hearsay statement, is not subject to any requirement that the declarant may have been afforded an opportunity to deny or explain. If the party against whom a hearsay statement has been admitted calls the declarant as a witness, the party is entitled to examine the declarant on the statement as if under cross-examination.

Adopted September 27, 2010, eff. January 1, 2011.

Article IX. Authentication and Identification

Rule 901. Requirement of Authentication or Identification

(a) *General Provision.* The requirement of authentication or identification as a condition precedent to admissibility is satisfied by evidence sufficient to support a finding that the matter in question is what its proponent claims.

(b) *Illustrations.* By way of illustration only, and not by way of limitation, the following are examples of authentication or identification conforming with the requirements of this rule:

    (1) Testimony of Witness With Knowledge. Testimony that a matter is what it is claimed to be.

    (2) Nonexpert Opinion on Handwriting. Nonexpert opinion as to the genuineness of handwriting, based upon familiarity not acquired for purposes of the litigation.

    (3) Comparison by Trier or Expert Witness. Comparison by the trier of fact or by expert witnesses with specimens which have been authenticated.

    (4) Distinctive Characteristics and the Like. Appearance, contents, substance, internal patterns, or other distinctive characteristics, taken in conjunction with circumstances.

    (5) Voice Identification. Identification of a voice, whether heard firsthand or through mechanical or electronic transmission or recording, by opinion based upon hearing the voice at any time under circumstances connecting it with the alleged speaker.

    (6) Telephone Conversations. Telephone conversations, by evidence that a call was made to the number assigned at the time by the telephone company to a particular person or business, if (A) in the case of a person, circumstances, including self-identification, show the person answering to be the one called, or (B) in the case of a business, the call was made to a place of business and the conversation related to business reasonably transacted over the telephone.

    (7) Public Records or Reports. Evidence that a writing authorized by law to be recorded or filed and in fact recorded or filed in a public office, or a purported public record, report, statement, or data compilation, in any form,

is from the public office where items of this nature are kept.

(8) Ancient Documents or Data Compilation. Evidence that a document or data compilation, in any form, (A) is in such condition as to create no suspicion concerning its authenticity, (B) was in a place where it, if authentic, would likely be, and (C) has been in existence 20 years or more at the time it is offered.

(9) Process or System. Evidence describing a process or system used to produce a result and showing that the process or system produces an accurate result.

(10) Methods Provided by Statute or Rule. Any method of authentication or identification provided by statute or by other rules prescribed by the Supreme Court.

Adopted September 27, 2010, eff. January 1, 2011.

Rule 902. Self-Authentication

Extrinsic evidence of authenticity as a condition precedent to admissibility is not required with respect to the following:

(1) *Domestic Public Documents Under Seal.* A document bearing a seal purporting to be that of the United States, or of any State, district, Commonwealth, territory, or insular possession thereof, or the Panama Canal Zone, or the Trust Territory of the Pacific Islands, or of a political subdivision, department, officer, or agency thereof, and a signature purporting to be an attestation or execution.

(2) *Domestic Public Documents Not Under Seal.* A document purporting to bear the signature in the official capacity of an officer or employee of any entity included in paragraph (1) hereof, having no seal, if a public officer having a seal and having official duties in the district or political subdivision of the officer or employee certifies under seal that the signer has the official capacity and that the signature is genuine.

(3) *Foreign Public Documents.* A document purporting to be executed or attested in an official capacity by a person authorized by the laws of a foreign country to make the execution or attestation, and accompanied by a final

certification as to the genuineness of the signature and official position (A) of the executing or attesting person, or (B) of any foreign official whose certificate of genuineness of signature and official position relates to the execution or attestation or is in a chain of certificates of genuineness of signature and official position relating to the execution or attestation. A final certification may be made by a secretary of an embassy or legation, consul general, consul, vice consul, or consular agent of the United States, or a diplomatic or consular official of the foreign country assigned or accredited to the United States. If reasonable opportunity has been given to all parties to investigate the authenticity and accuracy of official documents, the court may, for good cause shown, order that they be treated as presumptively authentic without final certification or permit them to be evidenced by an attested summary with or without final certification.

(4) *Certified Copies of Public Records.* A copy of an official record or report or entry therein, or of a document authorized by law to be recorded or filed and actually recorded or filed in a public office, including data compilations in any form, certified as correct by the custodian or other person authorized to make the certification, by certificate complying with paragraph (1), (2), or (3) of this rule or complying with any statute or rule prescribed by the Supreme Court.

(5) *Official Publications.* Books, pamphlets, or other publications purporting to be issued by public authority.

(6) *Newspapers and Periodicals.* Printed materials purporting to be newspapers or periodicals.

(7) *Trade Inscriptions and the Like.* Inscriptions, signs, tags, or labels purporting to have been affixed in the course of business and indicating ownership, control, content, ingredients, or origin.

(8) *Acknowledged Documents.* Documents accompanied by a certificate of acknowledgment executed in the manner provided by law by a notary public or other officer authorized by law to take acknowledgments.

(9) *Commercial Paper and Related Documents.* Commercial paper, signatures thereon, and documents relating thereto to the extent provided by general commercial law.

(10) *Presumptions Under Statutes.* Any signature, document, or other matter declared by statutes to be presumptively or prima facie genuine or authentic.

(11) *Certified Records of Regularly Conducted Activity.* The original or a duplicate of a record of regularly conducted activity that would be admissible under Rule 803(6) if accompanied by a written certification of its custodian or other qualified person that the record

    (A) was made at or near the time of the occurrence of the matters set forth by, or from information transmitted by, a person with knowledge of these matters;

    (B) was kept in the course of the regularly conducted activity; and

    (C) was made by the regularly conducted activity as a regular practice.

The word "certification" as used in this subsection means with respect to a domestic record, a written declaration under oath subject to the penalty of perjury and, with respect to a record maintained or located in a foreign country, a written declaration signed in a country which, if falsely made, would subject the maker to criminal penalty under the laws of the country. A party intending to offer a record into evidence under this paragraph must provide written notice of that intention to all adverse parties, and must make the record and certification available for inspection sufficiently in advance of their offer into evidence to provide an adverse party with a fair opportunity to challenge them.

Adopted September 27, 2010, eff. January 1, 2011.

Rule 903. Subscribing Witness' Testimony Unnecessary

The testimony of a subscribing witness is not necessary to authenticate a writing unless required by the laws of the jurisdiction whose laws govern the validity of the writing.

Adopted September 27, 2010, eff. January 1, 2011.

Article X. Contents of Writings, Recordings and Photographs

Rule 1001. Definitions

For purposes of this article the following definitions are applicable:

(1) *Writings and Recordings.* "Writings" and "recordings" consist of letters, words, sounds, or numbers, or their equivalent, set down by handwriting, typewriting, printing, photostating, photographing, magnetic impulse, mechanical or electronic recording, or other form of data compilation.

(2) *Photographs.* "Photographs" include still photographs, X-ray films, video tapes, motion pictures and similar or other products or processes which produce recorded images.

(3) *Original.* An "original" of a writing or recording is the writing or recording itself or any counterpart intended to have the same effect by a person executing or issuing it. An "original" of a photograph includes the negative or any print therefrom. If data are stored in a computer or similar device, any printout or other output readable by sight, shown to reflect the data accurately, is an "original."

(4) *Duplicate.* A "duplicate" is a counterpart produced by the same impression as the original, or from the same matrix, or by means of photography, including enlargements and miniatures, or by mechanical or electronic re-recording, or by chemical reproduction, or by other equivalent techniques which accurately reproduces the original.

Adopted September 27, 2010, eff. January 1, 2011.

Rule 1002. Requirement of Original

To prove the content of a writing, recording, or photograph, the original writing, recording, or photograph is required, except as otherwise provided in these rules or by statute.

Adopted September 27, 2010, eff. January 1, 2011.

Rule 1003. Admissibility of Duplicates

A duplicate is admissible to the same extent as an original unless (1) a genuine question is raised as to the authenticity of the original or (2) in the circumstances it would be unfair to admit the duplicate in lieu of the original.

Adopted September 27, 2010, eff. January 1, 2011.

Rule 1004. Admissibility of Other Evidence of Contents

The original is not required and other evidence of the contents of a writing, recording, or photograph is admissible if-
  (1) *Originals Lost or Destroyed.* All originals are lost or have been destroyed, unless the proponent lost or destroyed them in bad faith; or
  (2) *Original Not Obtainable.* No original can be obtained by any available judicial process or procedure; or
  (3) *Original in Possession of Opponent.* At a time when an original was under the control of the party against whom offered, that party was put on notice, by the pleadings or otherwise, that the contents would be a subject of proof at the hearing; or
  (4) *Collateral Matters.* The writing, recording, or photograph is not closely related to a controlling issue.

Adopted September 27, 2010, eff. January 1, 2011.

Rule 1005. Public Records

The contents of an official record, or of a document authorized to be recorded or filed and actually recorded or filed, including data compilations in any form, if otherwise admissible, may be proved by copy, certified as correct in accordance with Rule 902 or testified to be correct by a witness who has compared it with the original. If a copy which complies with the foregoing cannot be obtained by the exercise of reasonable diligence, then other evidence of the contents may be given.

Adopted September 27, 2010, eff. January 1, 2011.

Rule 1006. Summaries

The contents of voluminous writings, recordings, or photographs which cannot conveniently be examined in court may be presented in the form of a chart, summary, or calculation. The originals, or duplicates, shall be made available for examination or copying, or both, by other parties at reasonable time and place. The court may order that they be produced in court.

Adopted September 27, 2010, eff. January 1, 2011.

Rule 1007. Testimony or Written Admission of Party

Contents of writings, recordings, or photographs may be proved by the testimony or deposition of the party against whom offered or by that party's written admission, without accounting for the nonproduction of the original.

Adopted September 27, 2010, eff. January 1, 2011.

Rule 1008. Functions of Court and Jury

When the admissibility of other evidence of contents of writings, recordings, or photographs under these rules depends upon the fulfillment of a condition of fact, the question whether the condition has been fulfilled is ordinarily for the court to determine in accordance with the provisions of Rule 104(a). However, when an issue is raised (a) whether the asserted writing ever existed, or (b) whether another writing, recording, or photograph produced at the trial is the original, or (c) whether other evidence of contents correctly reflects the contents, the issue is for the trier of fact to determine as in the case of other issues of fact.

Adopted September 27, 2010, eff. January 1, 2011.

Article XI. Miscellaneous Rules

Rule 1101. Applicability of Rules

(a) Except as otherwise provided in paragraphs (b) and (c), these rules govern proceedings in the courts of Illinois.

(b) Rules Inapplicable. These rules (other than with respect to privileges) do not apply in the following situations:

    (1) Preliminary Questions of Fact. The determination of questions of fact preliminary to admissibility of evidence when the issue is to be determined by the court under Rule 104.

    (2) Grand Jury. Proceedings before grand juries.

    (3) Miscellaneous Proceedings. Proceedings for extradition or rendition; preliminary examinations in criminal cases; sentencing, conditional discharge or supervision; postconviction hearings; issuance of warrants for arrest, criminal summonses, and search warrants; and proceedings with respect to release on bail or otherwise, and contempt proceedings in which the court may act summarily.

(c) Small Claims Actions. These rules apply to small claims actions, subject to the application of Supreme Court Rule 286(b).

Adopted September 27, 2010, eff. January 1, 2011. Amended April 8, 2013, eff. immediately; Jan. 6, 2015, eff. immediately.

Rule 1102. Title

These rules may be known and cited as the Illinois Rules of Evidence.

Adopted September 27, 2010, eff. January 1, 2011.